Fossil Fuel Power

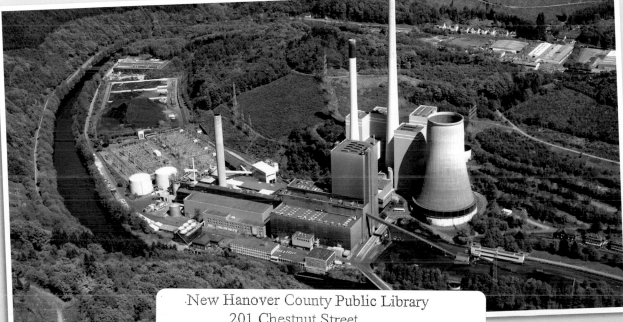

Richard and Louise Spilsbury

PowerKiDS
press.
New York

Published in 2012 by
The Rosen Publishing Group Inc.
29 East 21st Street,
New York, NY 10010

First Edition

Editorial Director: Rasha Elsaeed
Produced for Wayland by Discovery Books Ltd
Managing Editor: Rachel Tisdale
Designer: Ian Winton
Illustrator: Stefan Chabluk
Picture Researcher: Rachel Tisdale and Tom Humphrey

Library of Congress Cataloging-in-Publication Data

Spilsbury, Richard, 1963-
Fossil fuel power / by Richard Spilsbury and Louise Spilsbury. – 1st ed.
    p. cm. – (Let's discuss energy resources)
ISBN 978-1-4488-5261-1 (lib. bdg.)
1. Fossil fuels–Juvenile literature. 2. Fossil fuels–Environmental aspects–Juvenile literature.
I. Spilsbury, Louise. II. Title. III. Series.

TP318.3.S65 2012
333.8'2–dc22

2010046939

Photographs:
Corbis: p. 16 (Bill Ross), p. 17 (Reuters), p. 19 (Ivan Alvcarado/Reuters), p. 26 (Anders Debel Hansen/
epa); Getty Images: p. 18 (James P Blair/National Geographic), p. 20 (Alexander Miridonov/AFP),
p. 23 (Kazuhiro Nogi/AFP); NASA: p. 4; Shutterstock: Cover background (Bochkarev Photography),
cover main (Tonylady), p. 5 (Phillip Minnis), p. 7 (David Maska), 8 & imprint page (maksimum), p. 14
(Marek Mnich), p. 24 (Matthijs Wetterauw), p. 29 (LovelaceMedia); Wikimedia Commons: title page
& p. 11 (Dr. G Schmitz), p. 13 (Scott Meltzer), p. 15 (Jonathan Doti/US Air Force), p. 27 (Hans
Hillewaert), p. 28 (SPBer); Suncor Energy: p. 22.

Contents

The words in **bold** can be found in the glossary on page 31.

Fossil Fuels as an Energy Resource

Energy resources are substances that we use to do work. For example, energy resources include the wind we use to push along sailing boats and the wood we burn to make heat. Coal, gas, and oil are all fossil fuel energy resources. These fuels formed from the remains of living things that lived on Earth millions of years ago.

Energy Resources

Today 60 percent of all oil is made into gasoline and diesel, which is used to run the engines of cars, trains, airplanes, and ships. Many other machines, from cell phones to movie projectors, work using electricity. Power companies make, or generate, electricity using energy resources. Around two-thirds of all electricity used globally is generated using fossil fuels in **power plants**. The remaining third of electricity comes mostly from nuclear power, which uses the energy from reactions in special metal fuels, and hydroelectric power, which uses the energy in moving water.

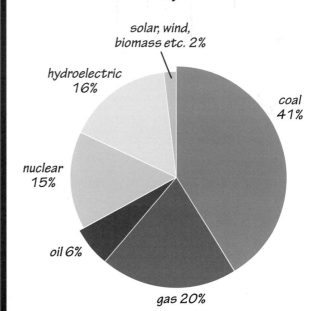

Global electricity from different energy resources

- solar, wind, biomass etc. 2%
- hydroelectric 16%
- coal 41%
- nuclear 15%
- oil 6%
- gas 20%

Images taken from space at night show which places around the world are using electric lights, and give an idea of the regions that use the most energy resources.

Power and Energy

Some people use the word "power" to mean electricity, but scientists use power to mean the rate at which energy is used or sent. Energy is measured in units called joules and power is measured in joules per second, or watts. A television needs about 100 watts of power to make it work, but a microwave needs over 1,000 watts or one kilowatt (kW). Big power stations make thousands of kilowatts of power at a time. We measure millions of watts in megawatts (MW).

Problems with Fossil Fuels

There are three main problems with using so much fossil fuels. First, they are a **nonrenewable** resource. Fossil fuels are running out because no more are forming. Second, burning fossil fuels releases waste gases. Some cause air pollution, but others, including carbon dioxide, are **greenhouse gases**. These trap heat in the atmosphere and cause **global warming,** which is having major impacts on weather and sea levels (see p. 14). Third, digging up and transporting fossil fuels damages the environment (see p. 18).

The massive engines needed to move heavy transport ships burn around a gallon of oil to move just several yards.

Why discuss fossil fuel power?

Governments, power companies, and individuals all around the world are looking to reduce the effects of using fossil fuels. They are using more **renewable** energy resources, such as wind, moving water, and sunlight, that will not run out. They are also using technological advances so they can use fossil fuels without damaging the planet. This book explores how we use fossil fuels to make power, their impact on the planet, and whether fossil fuels will be important fuels into the future.

What Is Coal?

Coal is a solid brown or black fuel. It is the commonest fossil fuel and is found in 50 countries around the world. The biggest amounts or **reserves** of coal are in the United States, Russia, China, and India.

Types of Coal

Coal is mostly made of carbon. There are several types of coal. **Lignite** is brown, soft, and contains 60–70 percent carbon. **Anthracite** is black, shiny, and hard, and can contain over 90 percent carbon. Coal with a higher proportion of carbon releases more energy when it burns. Grades of coal with less carbon contain more impurities, which burn releasing little energy or burn creating other, polluting substances.

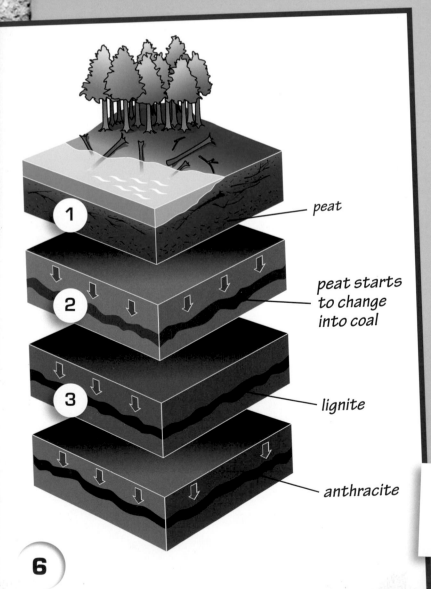

peat

peat starts to change into coal

lignite

anthracite

How Coal Formed

Coal formed mostly from forests that grew in swamps around 300 million years ago.

1 When the trees died, their remains built up in the water along with fallen leaves. The layer of plant remains was called peat.

2 The peat was gradually covered over with layers of soil washed off the land. The **sediment** stopped the peat from rotting. The weight of sediment layers at the top squashed those below into rock around the peat layer.

3 Gradually the peat was buried deeper underground, where high pressure and heat gradually turned it into coal in layers called **seams**.

Peat changed into anthracite over longer periods of high pressure underground, but into lignite over shorter periods.

Let's Discuss

Is open-pit better than underground coal mining?

Open-pit mining is when machines are used to scrape away a layer of earth and rock to dig up coal that is found near the surface. Most coal, especially anthracite, is buried tens to hundreds of feet underground. Miners dig underground mines to get at these deep coal layers.

Yes:

Cost and Safety
Removing soil and extracting coal from surface rock is quicker, safer, and cheaper than digging deep tunnels underground.

Large Amounts
Open-pit coal mining uses some of the largest machines on Earth, so tons of coal can be removed at a time.

Some open-pit coal mining machines have cutting wheels with 20 buckets where each can scoop up around 15 tons of coal at a time.

No:

Lower Quality
Most of the better quality anthracite coal, which pollutes less than lignite, is found deep underground.

Land Damage
Open-pit mining damages large areas of land surface whereas deep mining mostly affects rock hidden underground. For example, Hambach open-pit coal mine in Germany covers an area the size of 26,000 football fields.

Open-pit mining is easier, safer, and cheaper than deep mining, but the coal is often lower quality and the mining has a bigger impact on land.

Oil and Gas

Oil and gas formed in a similar way to coal, through high pressures and temperatures underground. However, these fossil fuels started as microscopic ocean animals and plants that were buried in sand and mud at the bottom of ancient seas. Their remains gradually turned into drops of oil and bubbles of gas that collected in spaces, or **pockets**, between rock layers.

Drilling for Fuel

In some places on Earth, oil and gas seep to the surface, but most of these fuels are trapped underground. Oil and gas companies drill deep holes through or along rock layers to reach oil and gas pockets. They use special drills with hard, diamond-tipped teeth to cut through the rock. Pressure underground often forces the fuels to the surface through pipes in the holes, or pumps suck the oil and gas out. Oil and gas are usually transported by long-distance pipes or in tanks on large ships called tankers.

Oil companies drill from platforms built on stilts to reach pockets of oil and gas trapped under the oceans. The flame is gas that is burned since it cannot be stored or controlled.

Crude Oil and Natural Gas

Oil straight from the ground is called **crude oil**. It is a mixture of different substances. It needs to be carefully heated up, or **refined**, in special factories to separate out the useful fuels such as diesel or gasoline. Natural gas is mostly made up of the gas **methane**. This gas is clear and odorless.

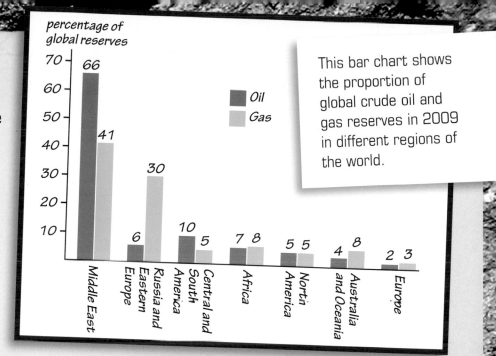

This bar chart shows the proportion of global crude oil and gas reserves in 2009 in different regions of the world.

Let's Discuss   Is gas a better energy resource than oil?

Yes:

Clean
Natural gas contains fewer impurities than oil, so burning it releases less air pollution. It also releases less carbon dioxide than oil.

Light
Gas is much lighter than oil, so it is cheaper to transport. It also contains more energy weight for weight than oil.

No:

Explosive
Natural gas catches fire and can explode much more easily than crude oil. If a gas container leaks, gas quickly spreads out across a wide space.

Greenhouse Danger
If methane escapes into the atmosphere, it stores about 20 times more heat than carbon dioxide, adding to the **greenhouse effect**.

On balance, gas is a better energy resource than oil but it is more dangerous to store and use.

How Power Plants Work

Most electricity is made in power plants, or stations, using either coal or natural gas as fuel. Oil is rarely used in power plants because it is more expensive than coal or gas.

From Coal to Electricity

1 Coal is broken into pieces and burned. The heat boils water, making steam.

2 The fast-moving steam has lots of **kinetic energy** that pushes against the angled blades of a **turbine**, which is shaped like a propeller.

3 The turbine spins and turns a machine called a **generator**. When coils of wire in the generator move around magnets, they generate electrical energy.

4 The steam that passes through the turbines in pipes is then cooled so it changes back into water to be heated up again in the boiler. Water used to cool the steam is itself cooled in giant cooling towers next to power plants.

Waste ash formed when coal burns collects in the bottom of the boiler. The ash is sometimes used to make roads or concrete.

Energy Conversion in a Coal power plant

boiler

turbine

generator

cooling tower

2

3

coal

1

4

water to cool steam

Energy changes from chemical energy in fuel to electrical energy in most power stations.

Using Gas

Power plants that use gas as fuel work in a slightly different way to coal power plants. A mix of air and natural gas is blown into burners using **compressed air**. The gas mix sets alight here and releases hot, powerful exhaust gases that spin large turbines with many blades. These turbines spin generators that produce electricity. Typical gas turbines weigh hundreds of tons and can generate about 80 MW of electricity. To do this, they burn 33 cubic yards (25 cubic meters) of gas, each second at around 1832°F (1000°C).

Coal power plants are often built near a river, as here, or a coast, because there is lots of water to make and to cool the steam from the turbine.

 CASE STUDY

Increasing Gas Power Efficiency

After passing through the gas turbines, the hot gas can be reused to create steam to turn other turbines and generators, making even more electricity from the fuel. This combined cycle technology is used in increasing numbers of power stations. At Irsching in Germany, the E.ON Kraftwerke company has developed the largest combined cycle station in the world. At its heart is an enormous gas turbine that can generate 340 MW on its own. Its energy output from fuel energy used, or efficiency, is 39 percent. Using a combined cycle, the efficiency increases to 60 percent, the electricity output increases to 540 MW, and far less carbon dioxide is produced per MW of electricity.

Using Oil for Transportation

There are almost 1 billion road vehicles and hundreds of thousands of aircraft and ships around the world. Nearly all of these vehicles use gasoline, diesel, and jet fuel, extracted from crude oil, for their energy.

How Vehicle Engines Work

Jet engines used on most airplanes work in a similar way to gas turbines in power plants. The spinning turbine sucks in air and heated jet fuel burns producing hot, fast gases behind the airplane. When the gases from the engine push on air, they create a force called thrust that moves the airplane forward. Airplanes are heavy machines that need powerful engines using lots of fuel to stay in the air. For example, a jumbo jet uses 5 gallons (19 liters) of jet fuel to fly just 1 mile (1.6 kilometers).

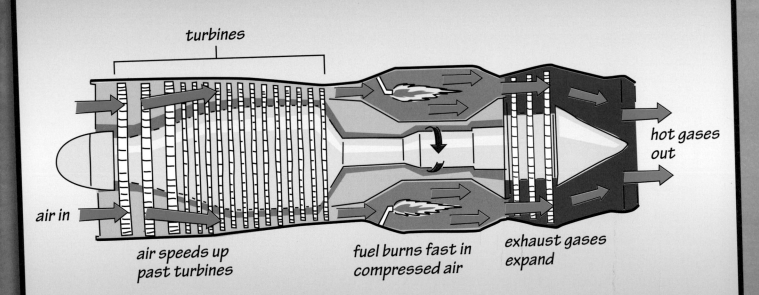

Inside a jet engine

turbines

air in

air speeds up
past turbines

fuel burns fast in
compressed air

exhaust gases
expand

hot gases
out

The different sized turbine blades in the jet engine press and speed up the moving air coming into the engine so it blasts through the gas burner.

Most vehicles have **internal combustion engines** that move their wheels or propellers. These engines contain several cylinders with sliding pistons inside. Burning fuel releases gases that expand to push each piston into its cylinder. Each piston is connected to a crankshaft with a rod. When a piston moves down, it turns the crankshaft a little. The crankshaft then pushes the piston up again because gases in the cylinder move out through a valve and into the vehicle's exhaust pipe. Pistons move up and down in sequence in the cylinders to rotate the shaft fast.

 **CASE STUDY**

Cars in China

In the 1990s, there were only around 250,000 private cars in China, but in 2009, there were 24 million. Each day, China uses enough fossil fuel in its cars to fill over 1 million Olympic-sized swimming pools. The number of cars has grown mostly because fast industrial development has created greater individual wealth, and China has such a massive population. The increase in cars in China, currently 10 percent each year, is faster than any other country. However, the number of cars per person in China is one-fiftieth of countries such as Canada and the United States. The U.S. uses the same amount of oil as China, India, Russia, Germany, and Japan, put together.

A heavily congested road on the outskirts of Beijing, China.

How Fossil Fuels Change the Atmosphere

The gases released through exhaust pipes from vehicles and through chimneys on power plants are forms of waste that have several harmful effects on the atmosphere.

Getting Warmer

The Earth stays warm enough for us to live on it because of the greenhouse effect. A third of the sunlight that hits Earth is reflected back into space, and the rest is stored by a layer of greenhouse gases in the atmosphere, including carbon dioxide. This layer of gases keeps the planet warm, but burning fossil fuels is significantly increasing the total volume of greenhouse gases. Most scientists agree that this is causing an increase in temperatures across the world. Global warming has many effects. For example, warmer seawater takes up more space in oceans, so sea levels rise and this threatens coastal settlements with flooding.

Damaging Rain

Fossil fuel pollution can create damaging **acid rain**. Acid rain forms when sulfur dioxide and nitrous oxide gases, released by burning coal that contains impurities, mix with water in the atmosphere. When acid rain falls to Earth, it can kill trees by preventing them from taking in nutrients from the soil. It can also harm wildlife in lakes and dissolve stone used in buildings.

The dead wood remaining from a once healthy forest in Poland killed by acid rain.

Let's Discuss

Does fossil fuel contribute more to global warming than other energy resources?

Yes:

More Carbon Dioxide
Fossil fuel power plants worldwide release 10 billion tons of carbon dioxide each year, more than from all the oil-powered vehicles on Earth.

Increased Effect
Carbon dioxide dissolves more slowly in warmer seawater. Therefore, global warming prevents ocean plants from using carbon dioxide in **photosynthesis**, and the warming effect increases.

No:

Less Methane
Flooding land to create hydroelectric reservoirs produces large amounts of methane. This traps more heat and stays longer in the atmosphere than carbon dioxide.

Damaging Biomass
Some farmers cut down forests to make space for **biomass** crops and this adds to global warming. Killing trees prevents photosynthesis, damaging soil releases methane, and burning biomass releases carbon dioxide.

The tall stack chimneys of the Dora power station, Baghdad, Iraq.

On balance, burning fossil fuels in power plants has a bigger impact on the atmosphere than other power technologies.

How Fossil Fuels Affect Health

Making fossil fuel power does not only affect the world's atmosphere. It also creates a range of health problems that affect many people globally.

Air Pollution

Coal, oil, and gas cause air pollution. When burned they can release harmful substances including carbon monoxide, nitrous oxide, poisonous vapors called PAHs, and tiny particles of soot, coal dust, and smoke. These substances can cause breathing problems and trigger asthma and even heart attacks in some people. Nitrous oxide and PAHs can react together with sunlight to form **smog**, a brownish, smoky fog that hangs over polluted cities with lots of traffic, such as Los Angeles, Beijing, or Mexico City. Smog contains high proportions of gases such as ozone that can cause lung damage.

Half of the population of the U.S. lives in areas with unhealthy levels of smog.

The Ozone Layer

When nitrous oxide rises up into the atmosphere, it can also damage the **ozone layer**. This is a layer in the atmosphere that is rich in ozone gas and acts like a sun filter. It stops harmful ultraviolet rays in sunlight from reaching the Earth. These rays can cause skin cancers and eye damage. With a thinner ozone layer, sun damage is more likely.

Mining and Drilling Hazards

Coal mining and oil or gas drilling are much safer than they were in the past, especially in more developed countries, but workers still face many hazards. Underground coal mines can collapse, methane gas found in pockets near coal seams can explode, and fires can rage underground for years at a time. Over the years, mine workers breathe in coal dust, which can cause lung disease. In China, over 4,000 coal mine workers die each year from various coal mining hazards. Oil and gas drilling is dangerous because these fuels catch fire easily and high underground pressures can blow out drills and underground pipes, injuring workers.

A rescue worker carries out a survivor from a collapsed coal mine near Hanoi, Vietnam, in 2006.

CASE STUDY
A Growing Mercury Problem

Scientists from the University of Alberta in Canada found in 2007 that mercury from dust released by coal power plants is poisoning fish in Lake Ontario when it falls to Earth and dissolves in water. Mercury levels are building up in animals in the lake. Small animals eat tiny amounts of the poison, fish then eat many of these animals, and predators such as trout and salmon eat lots of the fish. The fish develop problems with their nervous system and heart. When people eat these fish, they take in large amounts of mercury and can become sick, too.

How Fossil Fuels Harm the Earth

Fossil fuels do not only have an impact when they are burned. Getting fossil fuels from the ground and transporting them can also destroy and pollute areas of land and sea.

The Impacts of Mining and Drilling

Coal mines, especially open-pit, can destroy large areas of land and affect the lives of animals and plants living there. In 2009 in Maharashtra, India, a forest where tigers live was cleared to reach coal seams so there is now even less space for these endangered animals to hunt and find mates. Another problem is that waste soil and rock from mines often contains minerals that react with water to form acid. Rain can wash this acid into rivers and lakes, harming fish, snails, and other water animals. Acid and other harmful substances, such as lead, in mine waste can also pollute drinking water supplies.

Rain forest was destroyed to build the Urucu oil and gas well in Brazil, and the 373-mile (600-km) pipeline to the nearest city, Manaus.

Pipes and Tankers

There are 4,000 oil tankers and numerous long-distance pipes moving huge volumes of oil around the world. When tankers sink or pipes break, oil spills can cause major pollution disasters. For example, in 1991, a tanker spilled enough crude oil in Kuwait to fill 400 swimming pools. At sea, oil kills sea animals such as seabirds, because they swallow it or it damages their feathers so they cannot fly or remain warm in the water. When oil washes onto beaches and rocks, it harms coastal habitats and coastal tourism. Broken pipelines cause problems too, for example, in Colombia, oil from a broken pipeline polluted soil and water so badly that farmers were forced off their land.

Is transporting oil at sea too dangerous?

Yes:

Costly Damage
Oil spills pollute land for long periods and have long-term impacts on wildlife. Cleaning up is expensive and complex.

Targets
Oil tankers and pipes are possible targets for terrorists and also pirates seeking ransoms. In 2008, Somali pirates took control of an oil supertanker and demanded $15 million to return the cargo.

No:

Fewer Spills
Oil spills account for only about one-twentieth of the oil entering the oceans. More comes from water treatment plants. Newer tankers have stronger hulls to prevent spillage.

Only Option
Tankers are the only viable option for bulk transportation of oil. Transporting oil by land or air is too expensive and the spills could affect more people.

An oil company worker scoops up crude oil that spilled from a broken oil pipeline under San Vicente bay on the Chilean coast.

Transporting oil at sea does have its dangers, but at the present time, there isn't really an alternative.

The Cost of Fossil Fuel Power

The availability and price of fossil fuels, and therefore of fossil fuel power, are influenced by demand from fuel or electricity users and also by political situations around the world.

Power Price

The price of electricity depends on the price of setting up a power station and ongoing costs such as fuel and wages for power company workers. In general, fossil fuel electricity is currently cheaper than electricity made with any other energy resources. One reason is that fossil fuel technology is long-standing and cheap. For example, to build a gas power plant, it costs half as much as a nuclear power plant producing a similar amount of electricity. Another reason is that fossil fuel is relatively cheap because big power stations can buy fuel in bulk at low prices.

Supply and Demand of Oil

Oil is sold in units called barrels—approximately 42 gallons (160 liters). The price of a barrel depends on how much is being taken from oil reserves around the world. If oil companies supply more than businesses and individuals use, then the price drops. The price rises when the demand is greater than supply.

Special lifting cranes position a new gas pipeline carrying gas from Russia via the Baltic Sea to Germany.

Changing oil prices have many impacts. For example, supermarkets may charge more for food if fuel is more expensive for the trucks and airplanes used for transporting it. Changes in the global political situation also affect oil prices. For example, the international banking crisis from 2008 onward reduced wealth for many and because banks stopped lending money, many businesses closed. This lead to a dip in oil demand and caused the price of a barrel of oil to drop.

Let's Discuss

Can oil production meet rising demand?

Yes:

Oil Remaining
Giant oil fields such as those in Saudi Arabia can supply lots more oil of different grades at low production costs.

Agreements
International oil groups, such as the Organization of the Petroleum Exporting Countries (OPEC), agree on how much to produce to try to keep prices stable both for consumers and oil companies.

No:

Growing Economies
Increased wealth and car use in countries such as China and India is fast increasing demand for types of crude oil best suited to making vehicle fuels. Producers cannot supply enough to meet this demand.

Fewer Fields
Most oil fields in the world currently producing were discovered before the 1970s. Since then, very few new big fields have been found.

On balance, oil production cannot meet growing demand. An alternative will be needed in the future unless more oil is found.

Finding More Fossil Fuels

The coal that is left underground should last hundreds of years, but crude oil and gas reserves may only last about 50 years at current rates of use. Pollution issues aside, the easiest solution to the fossil fuel shortage is to find more. Oil, gas, and coal companies and scientists spend a lot of money and time exploring the planet for new reserves of fossil fuels.

Other Sources of Oil

Liquid crude oil is not the only source of oil. **Oil shales** are soft rocks found in large amounts in the United States, Estonia, and Russia. **Tar sands**, common in western Canada, are sands soaked in bitumen (tar). Both resources are mined and then crushed and heated to release the oil they contain. Extra reserves like this could produce around 4 trillion barrels of oil—enough to last 160 years at current rates of oil use. One downside is that the proportion of oil per ton of rock or sand is low, so extracting the oil is expensive, and leaves lots of polluting waste. Nevertheless, some oil companies are already starting to use these sources, and future technologies may make it easier and cheaper to extract them.

For tar sand to yield useful fuel, it is mixed with hot water and shaken in special machines to make the bitumen float away from the sand.

Frozen Gas

A much bigger source of fossil fuel is found in deep oceans and cold areas, such as Alaska and Siberia (Russia). **Gas hydrates** are tiny crystals of ice with ancient methane gas trapped inside. Scientists estimate that the gas hydrates so far discovered may contain twice the carbon energy of all the known fossil fuel reserves on Earth. However, mining the hydrates will not only be expensive in deep oceans, but could also release lots of methane into the atmosphere. This would increase global warming faster than releasing the same volume of carbon dioxide.

A worker from the Japanese Gas Association demonstrates how chunks of gas hydrate burn.

CASE STUDY   Coal-Eating Bugs

In water trapped deep underground, U.S. scientist Craig Venter and his team have found ancient bacteria that eat coal! The bacteria convert the coal into methane. Although the process has been demonstrated only in laboratories, Venter believes bacteria could be injected into coal seams to supply enough methane to burn in large gas power plants. The fuel should be cheaper than existing natural gas wells, because the coal would not actually have to be mined out of the ground to make the methane. Using more methane than coal would release as much energy to make electricity but less carbon dioxide.

Cutting Harmful Gases

If countries are to continue using fossil fuels, they need to find ways to reduce the damaging amounts of greenhouse gases and pollution that power stations and vehicles create.

Filters, Scrubbers, and Converters

Some power stations already have special filters inside their chimneys that absorb soot particles and **scrubbers** to remove polluting gases. Scrubbers include chemicals such as soda crystals that remove acidic gases including sulfur dioxide. New cars and many other vehicles have devices called catalytic converters fitted to their exhaust pipes that work in a similar way to scrubbers. Filters, scrubbers, and converters make a big difference to air pollution, but none of these devices gets rid of carbon dioxide.

Waste Less Heat

Scientists estimate that a power plant making 1,000 MW may lose 2,000 MW of power in the form of heat. The waste heat adds to global warming and can harm animals in rivers and seas. In some places, power companies **cogenerate**. This means they capture the waste heat to warm air and water in buildings. For example, Denmark gets over half of its energy by cogeneration. Cogeneration helps cut greenhouse gases because less fuel is used for heating.

When waste heat warms river water, water weeds grow faster, using up more oxygen. With less oxygen, water animals including frogs may struggle to survive.

Should power companies bury carbon dioxide?

Many power companies and countries plan to remove carbon dioxide from power plants and bury it underground. This is called carbon capture and storage, or CCS.

Yes:

Using Waste Space
Companies plan to use empty oil and gas pockets to store the gas. The carbon dioxide may even be injected down oil wells to help extract oil.

Clean Coal
In theory, CCS could remove up to 90 percent of carbon dioxide produced by coal power plants.

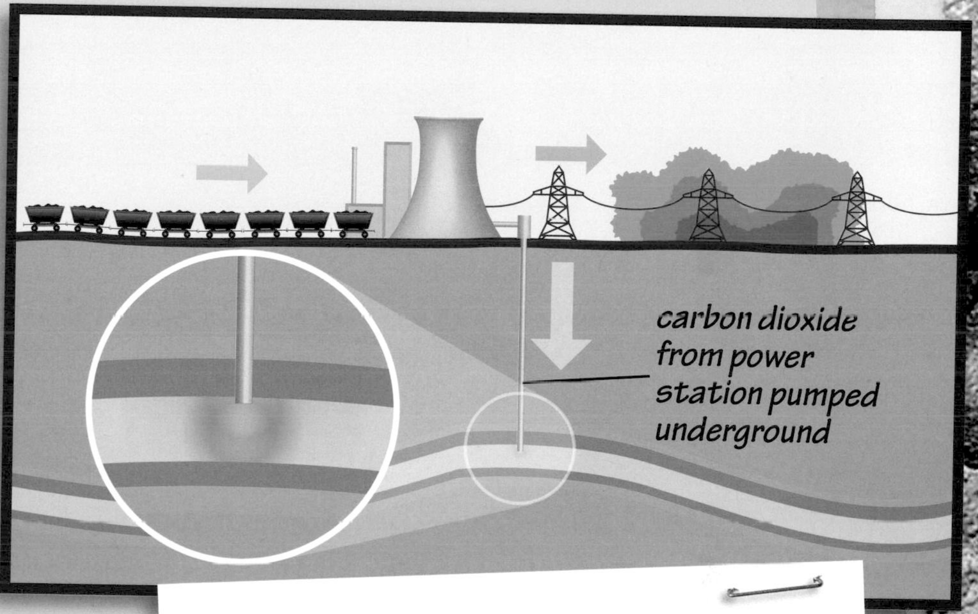

carbon dioxide from power station pumped underground

CCS will require vast and costly networks of pipes to get carbon dioxide underground.

No:

Cost
Building a network of pipes and pumps under power stations to transport carbon dioxide underground will make electricity more expensive.

Safety
The technology is unproven and may not be safe. For example, will the carbon dioxide leak from the ground over time?

On balance, CCS technology is a good idea, but it is too costly to reduce greenhouse gases at present. It also hasn't been tested enough.

Reducing Fossil Fuel Use

To help solve the problem of global warming, the governments of many countries have agreed together to cut the greenhouse gases they produce. Since they are committed to producing electricity and running vehicles to power their citizens' lives, the governments and power companies are looking for alternatives to coal, oil, and gas that are renewable and do not harm the atmosphere.

More Renewables

One solution many countries are trying is to generate more electricity using renewable energy sources—for example, building wind farms with turbines that use the power of moving air to make electricity, and solar farms that use the energy in sunlight. Some places, such as Iceland, are using geothermal power, which is heat from deep underground. In countries including the U.S., companies are burning crop waste, wood chips, and other biomass to create steam in power plants.

"Coal is 80% of the planet's problem.... The number one enemy is coal and we should never forget that."

Jim Hansen, director of NASA's Goddard Institute for Space Studies, 2009

In December 2009, around 100,000 people protested about global warming by marching through Copenhagen when world leaders at a UN conference were meeting to discuss cuts in greenhouse gas emissions.

Burning Together

Some power stations **cofire** or burn a mix of coal and biomass. The heat produced is not reduced by cofiring so the power station generates as much electricity as just using coal. However, apart from being renewable, burning biomass releases 20 percent less carbon dioxide and very little air pollution.

Let's Discuss

Should governments invest in renewable power?

Yes:

No Option
Fossil fuels are finite so governments have no option but to invest. The added benefit is new jobs creating renewable technology.

Cheaper
If power companies have to pay for the effects of global warming, fossil fuel power could become too expensive for consumers.

Offshore wind farms can be built at sea to make use of strong ocean winds.

No:

Unfair
Some people say it is unfair to subsidize renewable power, because it is generally too expensive at present to compete with fossil fuels.

Inadequate
Currently, renewables supply inadequate amounts of electricity. For example, wind power does not work on still days.

Renewables are the right choice for the environment but at present cannot supply enough power to meet global needs.

The Future for Fossil Fuel Power

Today, we rely heavily on fossil fuels. They are relatively cheap, plentiful, and there are no other energy sources that can fully and safely replace them. But we know fossil fuels cause global warming and pollution, and they are running out, so what is the future for fossil fuel power?

Future Demand

In 2009, the global population burned around 6.5 billion tons of coal to meet its electricity needs. To supply our demand by 2030, we will need to burn 60 percent more. The number of cars and number of air passengers are both set to double from 2010 to 2030. Matching fossil fuel supply with demand will require major investment by countries and power companies. For example, in the long run, more money will need to be spent on developing CCS, and extracting more fossil fuels including tar sands and gas hydrates from the planet. Many people concerned about global warming believe this money would be better spent on developing renewables to take over from fossil fuels. In the short run, we all need to use fossil fuels more efficiently. For example, power plants may cofire and cogenerate more than at present, and we will need to use more energy-efficient machines.

Schwarze Pumpe, Germany, opened in 2008, was the first coal power plant that could capture carbon dioxide, but by 2010, there was still nowhere to store the gas.

Power Change

Many scientists believe that we are coming to the end of the carbon age—the period since the Industrial Revolution when fossil fuels have supplied most of our power. Some believe we are on the brink of a new hydrogen age for transportation. Hydrogen cells are special batteries that release energy using liquid hydrogen as fuel, and emit only water vapor. The trouble is that to make hydrogen, from water, requires lots of electricity and this is mostly generated using fossil fuels. Other scientists think solar power will supply most electricity in the future, and that this could be used to make hydrogen.

Honda's FC Sport, a working model of a future performance car powered by hydrogen cells.

CASE STUDY — Designing Tomorrow's Airliners

In 2008, NASA ran an international competition for students to design more fuel-efficient airliners. These had to use less fuel while going as fast as today's airliners and have shapes that moved through the air with less air resistance. Airplanes use fuel at a faster rate when taking off, so the designs needed to be able to take off over short distances. The winning design by Georgia Institute of Technology had double wings that joined at the tip, providing low air resistance and electric motors for take off so it could run on less fuel.

Fossil Fuel Activity

What you need:
- 4 magnets (each about 2 x 3/4 x 2/5 in. (5 x 2 x 1 cm))
- 33 yards (30 meters) of magnet wire
- 1.5V/25mA light bulb with two short wires attached
- Cardboard strip, 12 x 3 in. (30 x 8 cm)
- Large steel nail, 3 in. (8 cm) long
- Tape
- Sandpaper
- Scissors

Make a Generator

Fossil fuel power plants, and most other power technologies, produce electricity using generators. All generators work by electromagnetic induction. This is when moving magnets cause electricity to flow in coiled wires. Here is how to make the simplest generator.

1 Make a box by measuring, scoring, and folding the cardboard with scissors as shown below. Tape it into shape.

2 Push the nail through the box from one side to the other. Wiggle the nail to widen the holes so that it can rotate easily.

3 Hold a pair of magnets on opposite sides of the nail (inside the box) until they pull toward each other and stay on the nail.

4 Tape one end of the wire, with about 4 in. (10 cm) sticking out, to one side of the box and wind the wire horizontally. The wire turns should be bunched closely together. Tape the other end, again with 4 in. (10 cm) wire sticking out.

5 Use the sandpaper to sand off the plastic coating on the wire ends. Twist them onto the wires from the bulb.

6 Rotate the nail as fast as you can, and see if the bulb lights up. It may help to do this in a darkened place since the light might be quite weak. How could you rotate the nail faster to make the bulb glow more brightly?

Cardboard box generator

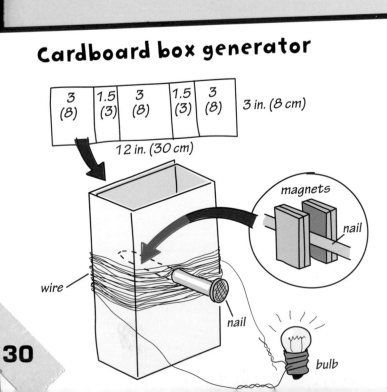

| 3 (8) | 1.5 (3) | 3 (8) | 1.5 (3) | 3 (8) | 3 in. (8 cm) |

12 in. (30 cm)

magnets

nail

wire

nail

bulb

Fossil Fuel Topics and Glossary

History
- Find out how fossil-fuel powered machines made the Industrial Revolution, from the late eighteenth century onward, possible.

Geography
- Sea level rise caused by global warming would affect millions of people living on coasts. Create a map showing places threatened by sea-level rise.

Design and Technology
- Cars in the 1970s were big and used lots of fuel because it was cheap. Design a car for the future with features to help it use less fuel as prices rise.

English
- Create a timeline from now to 100 years into the future showing possible impacts of dwindling fossil fuels.

Science
- Carbon is taken in by living things from the atmosphere and food, and collects in the ground when they die, sometimes as fossil fuels. Investigate the carbon cycle.

Glossary

acid rain rainwater with dissolved gases mostly from air pollution.

anthracite hard, slow-burning coal that produces lots of heat and little smoke.

biomass organic matter used as a renewable energy resource.

cofire to burn two types of fuel together to release energy.

cogenerate generate and use electricity and heat from the same process.

compressed air air pushed into a small space to give it greater potential energy.

crude oil oil taken from the ground.

gas hydrate type of ice containing natural gas.

generator machine converting mechanical to electrical energy.

global warming increase in the average temperature of the atmosphere and oceans.

greenhouse effect how gases in the atmosphere trap heat on Earth.

greenhouse gas gas such as carbon dioxide that stores heat in the atmosphere.

internal combustion engine engine producing power by burning gasoline or other fuel inside.

jet engine an engine producing forward movement by pushing gases out backward.

kinetic energy energy produced by movement.

lignite soft, fast-burning brown coal.

methane clear, odorless gas used as fuel.

nonrenewable energy resource such as coal that runs out because it is not replaced when used.

oil shale type of soft rock containing oil.

open-pit mining from surface rocks and soils.

ozone layer band of ozone gas in the atmosphere protecting the Earth from harmful radiation.

photosynthesis process by which plants make food using energy from sunlight.

pocket space in rocks where oil or gas builds up.

power plant (station) building in which an energy resource is used to generate electricity.

refine purify to create more useful substances.

renewable energy resource that is replaced naturally and can be used without running out.

reserve available supply.

scrubber device to remove polluting substances from exhaust gases.

seam thin layer of coal.

sediment sand and other small, solid pieces that are transported by and settle in water.

smog type of air pollution formed by reaction between smoke and gases in sunlight.

tar sand sand and clay naturally soaked in sticky, heavy oil.

turbine machine changing the push of water, steam, or other substance into rotational energy.

Further Information, Web Sites, and Index

Books

New Technology: Energy Technology
by Chris Oxlade
(Smart Apple Media, 2008)

The World of Energy: Understanding Fossil Fuels
by Polly Goodman
(Gareth Stevens Publishing, 2010)

What If We Do Nothing?: Fossil Fuels
by Jacqueline Laks Gorman
(Gareth Stevens Publishing, 2009)

Web Sites

Due to the changing nature of Internet links, PowerKids Press has developed an online list of Web sites related to the subject of this book. This site is updated regularly. Please use this link to access this list:
http://www.powerkidslinks.com/lder/fossil/

Index